Notes To The Psych Ward

Millicent Segwane

Published by Millicent Segwane, 2021.

<u>NOTES TO THE PSYCH WARD.</u>

By: Millicent Segwane

Author Contact details

- MillicentR.Segwane@gmail.com
- Instagram motivational page: https://www.instagram.com/culturedreasoning

The book you are about to read may not be appropriate for all audiences. Please read at your own discretion.

NOTES TO THE PSYCH WARD

First edition. January 14, 2021.

ISBN: 979-8215520239

Written by Millicent Segwane.

Preface

I know it's no excuse but I am just a 20 year old trying to wipe the tears
of the 8 year old that died inside of me, so forgive me if it feels like I
am just not here with you...
I have journeyed into the past trying to convince that little girl to set
me free but she sits at the bottom of my heart telling me I can't
abandon her like everyone else so forgive me when I seem distant
today, I am just trying to be there for that little girl that died inside of
me while you assumed she grew up.

\- **M.R.S**

Tired

I am going to do it...I am not sure when but I will do it
When the tears start choking me beyond what I can take,
When these people stop pretending to care,
When my heart gets so heavy that it drops,
When my headaches produced by tears get intense
When everything stops making sense
When I am tired of living under pretence
And everything is beyond tense
I am going to do it... – **M.R.S**

Escape

I don't know how much longer I can stay and the pharmacy provides
tickets to my escape – **M.R.S**

Aspiration

I wish I could be as strong as you think I am but I am not like the
people of this world...I can't grab a few words of inspiration because
for the longest time being gone has been my greatest aspiration
– M.R.S

Tallied

Karma found me when I was ready to change or maybe
God just tallied my sins and I reached my limits.
So many devils, couldn't send me to hell so they turned earth into a
burning furnace, melting in every corner.
I figured I open my heart and do what the good people do and love
maybe that would warrant me some grace, but all that just led to
disgrace and I remembered why I never took part in this race – **M.R.S**

Better place

Everyone is trying to make it somewhere in this life, man I am just
trying to make it out!
There's got to be a better place than here – **M.R.S**

Thin sparse

Searched till the ends of the earth and found the answer at the end of the bottle, now every night we sip the old me away and wake up in the morning wishing she spent the night because even though we both won't admit it, she is my knight, she used to be the reason that I tried, and now she stares at me and all I can do is cry because even though she won't say it, she blames me for what we are today, and the selfish side of me blames her because she was there too – **M.R.S**

Bleeding

I have scars that bleed till this day.
I have tears from ten years ago still finding their way down my face
Every memory is a grave and the present is the rain I walk through
– M.R.S

Acting

Putting on a show since 8,
Damn, while they were playing hide and seek,
My demons sought and found me.
Too young to dance with the devil so I figured I open a scripture to
stop me from being this awful creature.
On my knees pleading my case...
12 years later....still the same girl in need of some grace – **M.R.S**

Another day

Because no matter how much I need to be gone
So many want me to be here
So I take a pill to help me through another day - **M.R.S**

Difficult

I tried with these humans, I really did...
But when we're all trying to breathe the same air then everything
seems like a competition
And we forget that we're all just leading each other home. – **M.R.S**

Belief

On my own till the end because the big homie didn't want to be part
of the race.
Still a believer but the devil dances in my head and calls me his
daughter, so every night he comes to me and hands me the rope
because unlike everyone else he saw I couldn't cope, so now he's calling
me home, because right now I am abandoned and confused in need of
a muse, but I stopped searching because I always end up abused and
bruised – **M.R.S**

Thinking

I have thought about it you know?
The ropes, the pills, the razor, standing in front of a train...
I have thought about it...
– M.R.S

Curtains

It had nothing to do with healing,
It had everything to do with the fact that I couldn't blame you for
hurting me.
It had nothing to do with wanting to forget,
It had everything to do with the fact that what I won't forget was
somehow fake, staged and performed, I was the crowd, I applauded
you and although it was your performance...the curtain closed on me
– M.R.S

Drowning

It had nothing to do with the fact that every night I drown in my thoughts of you, so close to death I wish I could drown you in my pain, because it had everything to do with the fact that you caused it –
M.R.S

Trapped

My insides are dying to be let out
They're saying: "words on paper aren't enough Milli, you need to let us out!"
So I take that razor and I start tracing my body looking for an opening to set them free but every cut seems to invite more demons
They're jumping around in my head telling me to take my whole prescription tonight
– M.R.S

Lost pieces

I can't live with myself.
Every piece of me reminds me of a piece of me that I lost,
So I cut hoping that if I cut deep enough I might find a piece of me I
thought was gone
But the cuts have gone deeper and I am nowhere in sight
So I turned to the liquor but at the end of the bottle there's a note
telling me that what I am looking for is dead.
Hell, if a part of me is on the other side then my prescription provides
the means to get there
But I just can't bring myself to do it!
So I sit here, reading, writing, hoping and wishing that one thought
would just trigger me and I can be gone in the morning
So I can start searching for a piece of me that I might never find
– M.R.S

Boat

So desperate for you to take your words back
How can you stand there and tell me that the truth is you're no good
for me?
Is that what floats your boat? Because it sinks mine
And I am drowning and you're telling me in the middle of the ocean
that if I tried hard enough I could swim to shore
But how can you know that for sure? – **M.R.S**

Dying

Even with a life jacket, my heart's piercing through,
Just an inch closer and I am through
But maybe that works, because to be without you won't
– M.R.S

Mislead

If I didn't love you right then write a manual, I'll learn how
If I wasn't enough then tell me what you need and I'll provide
If it's beauty that you want then tell me which layers of makeup I
should apply
If it's boobs or booty, tell me which doctor can help
But if you found another, then just leave me in the middle of this
ocean and don't call for help
Because if I survive, I'll be living in pain
And if that works to ease your conscience
Then your love was in vain but somehow mine is still running through
my veins – **M.R.S**

Pained

There is so much pain you know? But I figured I keep it to myself...
Everyday someone tries to get me to open up and when I make that
mistake and let it all out, they tell me that my life isn't all that bad but
they will never feel what I feel,
waking up wishing you didn't,
having to forget what you wanted to be because life just made you
another being
and you're just stressed and depressed about everything and anything
so sad that sometimes you cry without cause
so pain filled that nothing can take it away
A few smiles here and there won't change the fact that before you close
your eyes to sleep you shed a tear
Trying not to speak because there is a knife in your windpipe
and you can't even breathe yet somehow still find yourself going
through life
There is so much pain you know?
So much and no one gets it. - **M.R.S**

Scars

Have you ever just forgotten yourself?
It's like I got knocked out along the lines of life and now I wonder how
I got here
I look in the mirror and I see scars and I have no clue on how they got
there
I see faces and people calling me their friend but truthfully I can't
remember how they even got here
– M.R.S

Coexisting

Happiness and pain coexisting, how can that be?
They exist so perfectly they take shifts
Happy Milli goes through the day and keeps everyone at ease
Hiding a piece of herself that she fears will bring nobody peace
Pained Milli goes through the night and fights all the demons present
On some nights she tries to give in so Happy Milli takes a sleeping pill
or two, some rest should do, anything to keep her restrained until the
morning so she can take over this body
Sometimes Pained Milli looks at Happy Milli and tries to choke her
while everyone is watching
A rope was the plan but Happy Milli made her realize, if you go... I go
too
So Pained Milli puts the chair away and hides the rope for another day
When happy Milli finally feels what she feels too. – **M.R.S**

Stubborn

Everyone wants to be here for me but once I tell them what I need
they tell me to kneel and ask the big homie for some blessings but I am
ashamed because the devil and his demons have taken residence in my
mind.
On some days I feel them eating at my soul
and on some nights they convince me to take my last breathe so they
can have my soul and all this pain is just so much!
I wish I wasn't stubborn and just fastened that noose
I have nothing left to lose.
Lost everyone I believed in, every shoulder turned into a rock and I
couldn't wipe my tears with the hard surface so I just showed smiley
faces day in day out,
hoping to cross the road a minute too late and it can all just be "an
accident" – **M.R.S**

Ran out

So pain inflicted by my peers, it's like they led me to a stream to drown
me
Family ties, everything broken before me.
They don't love me for me they love because the norm says blood is
love
So they love me for what runs through my veins,
As long as I breathe they will give me a roof over my head, pay all the
bills and invite me to every family gathering just so they can talk about
how different I am later on when I am gone.
My lecturers? They believed in me so they gave me all the help I
needed and I turned from grateful to feeling useless!
If I could not do it on my own then I don't see why I was doing it in
the first place.
The world's chasing trends and I stay behind trying to find something
to make me whole.
So drained of humanity and it's norms that I spent nights under a
bridge feeling at home
And the night wind gave me greater warmth than my blanket ever
could.
Gave my heart to him only to end up in a darker place than before,
He said sorry but that's not the code out of here,
And now everyone's telling me "it's just another guy"
And I look and smile thinking to myself...
But of course, it's just another hell reserved for me on this earth.
– **M.R.S**

Normal

I wonder what a new day brings for a normal person.
Does it bring rainbows and sunny skies?
Peachy weather or just a little bit of rain?
Ups and downs but both manageable?
I tend to think of myself to be far from the average person,
The normal person...
I am under the same sky as an average person,
But when it rains it pours for me while it's dry for everyone else
When the night comes it seems to stay longer for me,
I figured the average person needs to sleep,
But I am far from dreamland
If my doctor forgets to slip in a pill or two,
Enough to make me sleep, but not too much to kill me
I wish he was empathetic
I wish he could see that just a little bit more would be enough and that
less was driving me crazy,
One or two? Still far from the average person. – **M.R.S**

Storm

I've been praying to get my date of expiration
Because I am sour now, I am a cup no one can drink from
I am that well that no one can throw coins in
I am that genie that no one makes wishes to
And my hand is not the one that can walk you through the storm
The world is experiencing a drought, people on their knees praying for
rain
If I could just let everyone into my world because here it rains and it
pours – **M.R.S**

Ghost

"What ever happened to the old you?" they ask so I turn my back and I
find her standing there daring me to speak,
she's screaming at me:
"Tell them! Tell them what you did!"
I stand up ready to shut her up but my hands go through her mouth
And I realize the old me is gone, she's just a ghost screaming to be
brought back to life because her reincarnate is trying to take them
back to where she currently resides – **M.R.S**

Knife

I can't tell you when it started hurting
I can't put a date to the pain because it feels like all my life I had a
knife stuck in my heart – **M.R.S**

Saying

Some nights I sit with my blankets wrapped around me and I look to
the ceiling and I imagine a voice calling my time of death
I hear beeping around me as my lifeline slowly cuts
I see my mother shaking me, pleading to the heavens that I wake
I see my eyes wide open as I take my last breath and before a tear
comes down
I put my hands over my eyes and go to sleep – **M.R.S**

Aware

I went back in time looking for you
The old you, I wanted that girl that smiled effortlessly
I wanted that girl that thrived even when life was hard,
I wanted that girl that needed only her love to continue this life
I found her, I saw her standing in the far distance of our past and I
realized she died young,
8 is such a small age to lose yourself, while mates made mud cookies
you stared at them wondering if your lack of participation made you
different.
You were a living ghost,
They all saw you but never through you – **M.R.S**

None

And one day I just woke up a different person
I don't know, I can't honestly tell you how I got here
I went from crying myself to sleep to feeling nothing at all
They say it hurts until you feel nothing
So I grab that razor and I start cutting until I feel something
But I still feel nothing,
It's like I went on a journey to the Promised Land and once I got there
I wished I could turn back
I try to smile, maybe that is what my present is telling me,
It's telling me maybe my past just led me to a better place,
So I let my dimples show, and they're deeper than before
And everyone says I look happier than before
Dressed by happiness but my scars are what I am still trying to address
But my heart's empty, my eyes are cried out, nothing can hurt me now
and nothing can please me too,
So I stare in the open trying to put two and two together
But I am afraid that all along I was being led to nothing at all,
Spent nights trying to find a better place, a place that replaces the pain
But they just took it, and didn't replace it for me...
This is me now,
And this is what it's like to be empty. – **M.R.S**

Grace

Sometimes I wonder if the big homie brought me this far just to drop me off here,
Let the devil take over and lead me to my actual home
Every night I think of my past and I am afraid that all along I was the daughter of the serpent
Sin was my life, and repentance just found me a little too late
And I am constantly falling short of grace – **M.R.S**

Obscure

All I needed was a picture of what lied ahead of me
If I liked what I saw then this road wouldn't be as bad as it feels
But I stand here, with no clear vision of tomorrow,
They tell me if I just stopped crying then my eyes would cease to be
blurry and I could see the road ahead clearly
But I don't think I can make it to my destination without this pain
It has brought me this far
On some nights it choked me until I yearned to be gone
And on some nights it was the only thing reminding me that I am
alive
And as I stand here on this road, it's the only thing telling me that
maybe getting to the destination isn't the answer
It's whispering in my ear that the end isn't meant for me because not
everyone makes it to the finish line and that's okay – **M.R.S**

Race

Spent years looking for grace,
Any strength to help with this race,
But life isn't for everyone...
That's the hard truth I had to face. – **M.R.S**

Humanity

On some days I want to be held so tight that I start believing in the good of this world
So tight that I finally feel like in the midst of all this chaos I have found my home
But then I move away from that idea when I remember you...
Your arms used to hold me safe from the world and your presence made me believe in the good of humankind
But now every time I think of you, I turn to look at the rest of the world and I am just drained of humanity – **M.R.S**

Alone

There's so much pain you know?
After all this time it still loams over me like it just arrived
And I am wishing that it would just stop because it reminds that you
are no longer with me – **M.R.S**

Cowardly

Every night I think of how to be gone
And when I wake up in the morning I sadden knowing I have not
figured it out yet
Or maybe I know how to be gone I am just scared of what will happen
if I survived
Will they forever be looking at me through pitiful eyes?
Will they pay attention to the smallest things I do?
Will my health be affected so much that I wish with every breathe I
take that I would just be gone?
Will I suddenly wake up and see the good in this world because from
where I am standing there has got to be a better place than here...
I heard about the son of man and his kingdom
They say there reigns peace and so I pray every night that he would
grant me that on earth
Because I know if I take myself out then hell is where I am headed
Because I have been in the presence of the devil for so long that he
calls me his daughter – **M.R.S**

Zzz

I have permanent zzz in this life, I am sleeping on it or better yet
sipping through it
The less I could control and remember the better, even if I had too
much that my guts tried to escape the following morning.
It just didn't matter anymore
Whether I fucked around and hanged myself in hopes to cope...it
didn't matter
My pain didn't matter because...
I didn't matter... – **M.R.S**

Dramatic

I didn't want to be another person,
This is me now and this is what it feels like to be broken
I didn't fantasize about being happy because I felt that would mean
that I was not sad enough
I didn't think to put myself together because that would mean I wasn't
broken enough
I chose to ignore the light because if not then that would mean I
didn't stay in the dark long enough
I didn't want to be strong because then that would mean I wasn't weak
enough
I didn't fantasize about you coming back because that would mean
you didn't hurt me enough
I didn't want to get better, because if I found my way back to sanity it
would mean I wasn't lost and all I felt was false and my reaction would
be deemed "dramatic". – **M.R.S**

Fault

I was too ashamed to admit it but...
I know now that all along I was the problem
I could have never loved,
I could have cared less,
I could have never showed up,
I could have just turned a blind eye,
I could have just closed myself off,
I could have been an introvert,
I could have walked away,
I could have made a better decision,
I could have thought about it more
I could have taken a different route...I could have but I did not
And it's no one's fault but my own. – **M.R.S**

Forgotten

In some ways I am a princess that needs saving
In some ways, a kiss from a frog is the answer
In some ways, I am that girl locked in that tower
In some ways, an evil step mother would be a blessing
In some ways, I am the one standing behind that gun
In some ways, I am the one that put a fork in my heart
In some ways, my death seems near
Because in all the ways possible...I am in need to be gone and
forgotten. – **M.R.S**

Sentenced

I can't even tell you what I feel,
I can only tell you what the feeling makes me do
And right now it has me walking through life with a fork in my chest
I am bleeding to my destination
It has me thinking that murderers are generous, how can anyone ever
get mad for being relieved of this burden called life?
How can you sentence someone who freed someone that got
sentenced to breathe? – **M.R.S**

Burden

Every breath I take feels like a curse,
To know I am alive is a burden
How can anyone expect me to carry this body?
Make it smile, feed it, bathe it, take it to work, buy it car, make it sleep,
blah blah blah – **M.R.S**

Self-love

One more speech about self-love and I am done for
Tired of people seeing my wrists and telling me I need to love me
more
If I ever cared about anything in this world, that thing is me
And maybe the problem lies there
The fact that I cared so much about myself that I spend years trying to
perfect my craft and now it's a problem when my pain has caused this
rift and I am fighting me on a daily
But I am still the one I love and care for
Made plans to be gone, but I stayed for me
Still hurting with no escape so I take the razor and decorate my walls,
Some red paint should do
And sometimes it takes a deep path to get the darkest red
My darling, self-love has never been this...deep. – **M.R.S**

Box

The world is my casket
I died a long time ago,
My soul's lost in this box... – **M.R.S**

Miracle

I didn't share my pain so that they would understand, no
I hoped by some miracle they would feel what I felt...
I didn't want anyone to "relate", No...
By the time you relate it's too late,
The poem I wrote yesterday isn't the person I am today,
What I felt yesterday is not what I feel today
I was possessed when you read the first poem but now?
You got Lucifer putting words together and making you feel the heat
Welcome to my hell. – **M.R.S**

Script

I've been losing everything and everybody I believed in
My faith must have been misdirected
Sometimes I wish I could turn my life into a movie
Maybe I would feel better if all of this was scripted – **M.R.S**

Funeral

I used to be in love with being alive
now I look at these pills and just figured I'd die
Thoughts of a funeral, me in that casket.
– M.R.S

Bible

I spent years looking for a better place than here,
So I turned to the scripture and it directed me above
But it's not an easy ticket in there, turns out I gotta actually care about
everything right here – **M.R.S**

Discouraged

On some nights I feel nothing,
I stare at the ceiling trying to remember all the pain but the memories
just seem like another clip played to the point of annoyance, and I get
frustrated that Pain has left the headquarters
But on some nights? Pain runs the shows
He grabs me by my memories until I choke
Pinches on my scars until they bleed again
Puts his foot out and lets me trip all over the place
Hands me the rope and dares me to get out of this place
And if my stubborn streak starts he puts that mirror in front of my
face and yells "Pathetic!" – **M.R.S**

Space

I couldn't care anymore, it used to be second nature to care about every little thing now I have to remind myself to do it and it seems like too much work
Empathy just wasn't something I could harbour anymore
And love just seemed like something no one deserved to get from me
So I stay in my own little space hoping everyone just stays away from me – **M.R.S**

Playlist

Damn I ran to the music for help but the more I relate
I realize the artist's too late
Nothing can save me, I will probably make a playlist
Something to play when I drown in those pills tonight. – **M.R.S**

Sudden

I didn't want to be this person...
You think I woke up one morning hating every corner of this earth?
You think I just flipped a switch and never gave a damn?
You think I took just one look at the world and said fuck it?
Honey...hating myself takes years of experience
To give the least fucks takes thousands of knives behind my back
To sleep walk through life takes thousands of pills – **M.R.S**

Baker

I didn't have to use my heart to be heartless
I just gave it to a human and expected him to carry it like an egg, he
was my egg until he tripped and fell into flour and baked the next girl
the best cake and left me with shells - **M.R.S**

Benefit

Damn, that was my ticket to hell
Now every time I hear the word love,
I think burning, I think tripping, I think falling,
I think two horns and a fork in my heart,
I think everyone benefits from my pain
– **M.R.S**

Guilty

The bible says "you have not because you ask not"
But God I keep asking, I don't shy away from my requests and I never
believe they are too big for you to grant
I am a sinner who is probably going to sin again, but your mercy and
grace will be just the same,
Lately I been feeling undeserving and your silence confirms it, and I
am afraid that all along you were counting my sins
Put them in a box and tallied them on paper, many cups runneth over
with blessings, my runneth over with sins
I see the lack of blessings and I wonder if luck is a blessing as well
because if so then I am screwed,
I realized I ran out of luck when every heart I broke stopped loving me
despite my faults, and my cup of blessings became empty when my sins
crashed the database, no memory was enough to keep all my wrongs
on record and now my prayers are sounding like a broken record and
now I wonder if my sorry is enough to find my way back to you
because back then my only faith was prayer, with every sin I found
myself regretting it, but now I sin and I feel no remorse,
sometimes I want to blame you but then I blame him, his lack of love
for me when all I had was pure intentions turned me into this sinner,
his lack of love for me turned me into this nightmare,
his lack of love for me...I wish he told me he wasn't ready to love like I
was, because maybe then I would still be an angel, but now I carry a
fork and every heart I meet is met with my wrath,
I am raising hell, even the devil has had enough of me but when they
hurt you like they hurt me, you turn into something the devil envies

...my cup of sins runneth over, had me thinking the sea could carry my wrath but now everyone is drowning in my flood of anger.

– **M.R.S**

Pieces

Every day feels like I am making it through because my pain has
become my new normal
Everyone thinks I am getting back to the old me so they don't offer a
shoulder because the old me was strong
I sit here surrounded by all the pieces of me that they broke and I find
comfort in my brokenness – **M.R.S**

Fake

They all want to get close to me but every time I hear the words:
"I am here for you" I think fake,
I think everyone just wants to make sure that when I finally decide to
cave they can stand at my grave and console themselves with the fact
that they said those words – **M.R.S**

Lazy

Every time I hear the words "you are strong" I think lazy,
I think people just don't have the energy to see me through so they
pass off a few words hoping I catch on and make it through – **M.R.S**

Emptiness

Because when the pain first got here all I needed was for it to be gone
and so I figured I down my prescription and be gone but now I can't
go
There is no other place where I can feel what I feel
This is me now...and this is what it feels like to be empty. – **M.R.S**

Prophecy

Not prophetic but I see a goodbye written in cursive
A couple bottles on the night stand looking to the roof and cursing
"Fuck this, fuck that"
Don't worry though ama die happy
Smiling every day, but the ocean's filled with her a.m. tears
Damn, now the front row is filled with tears, black is the theme,
Celebrating the life of someone who hated every minute of it
You didn't think today you'd be here
Sending her to her final resting place, hoping she finds peace with the
angels
But the devil is her father,
He was there with the fork, and he used it to stab her
Told her these people don't care about you baby I came to get you
She can't go to heaven now, because she's paying for all the times she
danced with the devil
The devil don't want her though because her service was held in a
church now she's standing at the doors of heaven wanting to turn back
time, but it is too late now, the end of the bottle was her finish line.
Racing in her mind, trying to turn back time, tear that goodbye up,
Throw the pills down the toilet and flush it down with all the pain
Can't you see with suicide you have nothing to gain?
Let's address that pain sweetie
Get on your knees, all you need is some grace - **M.R.S**

Mercy

Sometimes I wish my mind could get tired instead of my body
Because thoughts from years ago still find me in the a.m. and every day
they introduce new ideas
And produce more tears and I am left at the mercy of a pill hoping it
would take it all away – **M.R.S**

Thoughts

The pain? I don't mind
It's the only thing I know
But I wish I could silence the thoughts because they remind me of
how I got here
– M.R.S.

No...

I don't look back because it's my past that I hate and if the future
seemed bright I would pick myself up and keep going but I choose to
stay stagnant, because every step just leads to my grave and I see myself
feeling nothing on the other side
so I stay fixed in this pain, I can't feel anything but hurt and I am
scared to kick the chair from below my feet because I fear ending up in
a place where I feel nothing at all
Some people choose to feel nothing at all
So they take those pills and when the morning comes they are gone
But I fear the unknown so I throw away the pills hoping the pain
consumes me through it all. – **M.R.S**

Smudged ink

You just don't know what you did to me,
If it wasn't for being this drained I would write it all on a page,
Scribble the scars and a few blank spaces there should do
Smudged ink...
On some days I drown,
On some nights I dance with the devil
Sometimes I lurk and search for you in all the places that I might have
lost you
Her arms, by her lips, in her eyes...but I don't see you there
I feel you in my heart and it's crazy that maybe that's where I lost you
Searched for you amongst these people,
I didn't know all along you were locked away in my heart
Trying to break free, now my heart's finally breaking, and I am afraid
your freedom leaves me pained and caged – **M.R.S.**

Age

Man I wish I could just age!
Taking myself out isn't the answer,
So I figured I put a few years on my name
Wishing old age can be the ticket to a better place. – **M.R.S**

Reaching out

I figured I stopped hiding behind my pain,
I figured I stopped smiling and frowned accordingly
They asked me what's the matter and I decided to open up
Now my wounds are out in the open, my pain? belittled
Everybody wanna put me in a corner like a kid,
They say: "Cry all you need, as long as you build a bridge over that
pain and get over it"
They say: "do what you gotta do to get past this, baby you're better
than this"
So I sank back into my hole, and figured I'd go through it alone
Because they see the tears, not the pain,
I just need a hand, I reached out, a couple cries for help
The slit wrists on my story weren't from the net, that was my hand
That girl hanging from the ceiling wasn't for awareness, I was just
saying my goodbyes
I didn't need to talk, I needed someone to show me the way
Show me the ropes, but they turned blind so I reached for that rope –
M.R.S

Peeping

Damn, tell me what the fuck is hope?!
When you're on your knees, but everything still shatters so you're
thinking of taking dope.
When the pain cuts so deep, and you peep but everyone's gone deaf!
Lord can you hear me speak?! I just pray you're making a plan
Because if I am on my own, a note by the nightstand and a few pills
too late is my fate – **M.R.S.**

Headestone

Damn, Suicide came to me and told me your lack of love was the bait,
he knew how to get to me
And now I am sitting here, rope or pill?
How I am going out is the debate
My death will be the last statement I ever make
Because it's like I am talking to the walls with every word I spit,
So you deserve to talk to the headstone and feel what it's like to cry
and wonder why that motherfucker don't reply! - **M.R.S**

Premeditated

I have been feeling like I need help lately
The doctors knew it too
Now the pharmacy is the park I walk through to find my way to joy
But I am so medicated,
One more pill and they will say my death was premeditated – **M.R.S**

Speak

Shouldn't have scribbled my pain on paper,
Translated my pain to a sentence worth reading
Because now I feel selfish,
Feeling like my pain is making happy people feel like they're relating
Sinking them deeper than my cuts,
It makes me sick to my guts!
My words can never be translated to happiness so the kids sit on the net and catch my feelings
They feel like they know what I am going through so when I fantasize about being gone in these lines they are drawn to me, so they don't mind when they drown with me,
But I wanna take it all back, be that kid that just fell from that roof
But it's too late, I took a pen, now they relate. – **M.R.S**

Racing car

I feel like our love was a hype train
It went so fast, everything happened now
Anything later than that would have been tragic
But that's the thing, maybe tragedy should have been the aim
Because I felt like you were a race car I was driving
Trying to move past all these couples and show them that we are the best
Took my eyes off the road, feeling cocky and I believed I could handle you
Everyone told me I was going too fast
"Milli you need to slow down"
Painted a picture they understood
So I hit the brakes trying to slow us down,
Because I thought it was too soon for us to make it to the finish line
But something went wrong, it seems I was faster than I thought
Do you know how hard it is to slow down a fast car without crashing?
We hit the wall, I ended up in ICU and you at the panel beaters getting beat back to perfection
While the machine beeped me out of this life,
We didn't make it to the finish line, me without you? Don't you see that I can't be?
Now the men in white are whispering "we tried our best, but she's gone"
So they put that cloth over my face and send me to another place
While you prepare to take your next race. – **M.R.S**

Options

Sat at the bar every night
hoping alcohol poisoning would be my knight
– **M.R.S**

Freed

Maybe life just isn't for everyone
But we are just so afraid to admit it because we will lose the ones we
love, but isn't that just selfish?
Wanting someone to take another breath for your sake
Even though you know that with every breath they take it feels as if
they are being punished for being here?
Sometimes I wish my loved ones could just release me,
Tell me "Milli it's okay, we know life just isn't for you so you can go, we
promise to be okay"
But every time I fantasize about being gone they tell me there is more
to this life
And I sink back into my little hole because I know that there has got
to be a better place than here...
If they could just release me and the big homie just accept me
regardless of how I ended up at his doorstep. – **M.R.S**

Enough

I was afraid all along that my karma would tweak for hella long
But if you are who they say you are then my sins were forgiven before
the pain
So I trusted the process,
I treated faith like an investment and I waited for my returns
Because for me hope didn't work like a pyramid scheme,
You put everything in and get nothing back,
But I looked at my situation and I felt I had been scammed
But then again I was the fraud,
The motherfucker that put my faith on a timeline
Every minute betting on you to show me you are real,
Every second delayed
I turned on you,
My prayer went from "gimme my daily bread" to "you can keep that
shit"
Acted out in the open, cursed to the heavens and when I saw them on
their knees I laughed and went "hey, there goes another puppet"
But I miss having you pull me by the strings because even though I
turned my back, you always showed up
And I was glad you showed up when you did and not when I asked
So I figured I light a candle up and seek forgiveness for my past
But I didn't see the blessing because my present was the same and I
knew then that I had no one but myself to blame
Wanted to walk away from you because I couldn't see how we would
work

A father and a daughter somehow estranged, won't admit it but it felt
strange to know that after all these years our relationship somehow got
strained
That I would let my rage lead me to a path where I had enough of you
The pain was a blessing and I knew it too, which is why on the day I
felt it move I would find ways to ignite it back
Said I don't need you but when tears go down my face I asked you
"where you at?"
And I hope my actions don't confuse you because I need you,
I just need you to tell me what to do – **M.R.S**

Hope

The little girl in me is keeping me alive
Every time I contemplate taking that rope,
She pulls my hand and tells me to jump rope – **M.R.S**

Miracle

I do not really want to be gone you know?
But every night I talk to the devil and he tells me how to be gone
And before I sleep I light a candle and ask for forgiveness from the big
homie but he doesn't reply and I am left thinking this is what I get for
even sitting down with the devil
But I feel the big homie misunderstood what he saw
The devil set the table, I sat there just to turn him down
Every night I cry wondering what it is that I failed to ask forgiveness
for
I read testimonies about how the big homie pulled through and
granted many miracles and I am left on the side-lines and I am
convinced now more than ever that I have fallen short of grace
So I take this rope, I take this pill but I fear that the big homie is still
listening and that I will survive my attempt
It's like even in his silence I feel his presence
I wish I shut him out completely so I can just be gone and don't have
to watch how he helps everyone but me
On some days I feel that my miracles had been granted but someone
stole them from me
And the devil laughs telling me that I chose to eat at the wrong table
so I continue,
Pen and paper, every night just trying to compensate for the big
homie's silence and trying to shut the devil up
But I am afraid that one day I will finally give in and let the devil take
me home. – **M.R.S**

Forward

The devil is a step ahead of me
When they put me on the pills I figured that was the solution to my
pain but every night the devil whispers in my ear that the pills are just
a way to end it all
He tells me: "If you just take the whole prescription, I promise it won't
hurt"
But the one I kneel to is telling me to hang on and I am caught
between the two
Because the other provides his word and the other hands me the pills
and tells me heaven is at the end of the bottle
Got me thinking about the time when I was little,
When the pain got too much my grandma's arms were my peace
Now I sit with this bottle thinking maybe the devil's right,
Just down it all and go see nena
But the one with the scriptures is telling me nah
He's telling me that I should seek him first so I went to the building
where his people gather
Went on my knees but I had nothing to say so I stood there with tears
down my eyes hoping that conversation was enough
But that was ten years ago and his silence matched mine,
Got me wishing I could turn back time
Go back to the alter and say what I actually needed
Talk to him like his blessings were on the menu for me to choose from
So I could ask for peace with a side of disappearing act,
Have them forget me and let me exist in the woods by myself
Just me and this pen
At night I hold my head frustrated thinking about that day,

The one chance I had with the big homie face to face and my mouth
just wouldn't find the words to grant us grace
So I listen to the devil, I take this fork and accept the fact that I cannot
continue with this race. – **M.R.S**

Sky

I should be gone by now
I should have made it to the other side by now
Holding hands with the devil and dancing through hell
Thinking about how I should have stayed longer and maybe been
granted grace from above
And maybe that is why I am still here...
I know where I belong, how else could I not know when the devil calls
me his daughter?
So I stay another day, looking to the heavens waiting for some grace so
I can finally finish this race. – **M.R.S**

Home

What if I just said fuck this life I don't want to be here?
What if I just stood at the edge of a cliff and just one more step we can
put an end to it all?
What if I just drank the bleach, a quick drink out of this ditch?
What if the razor went deeper than just a stitch?
What if I forgot that these pills make me itch?
What if I just fasten that noose?
What if I just stopped being a coward and just fell from that roof?
What if I stopped fantasizing and just did it?
What if I just write that note, can't speak from my heart so I'll just
leave with a quote...
"Them people killed me daddy, I'm coming back home"- **M.R.S**

Cycles

Sometimes I don't want to write
I am scared someone will read and be like "this can't be her life"
I wanna add dates to my work but I can already see my friend going
"But that day we had a blast"
I am always the light of the party, but am I having fun? Not hardly
Sometimes I don't want to write but the pen knows the real me
I could never find comfort in talking because they are listening to be
in the loop not because they care
So I put on a smile and be that girl that they need me to be
If I wore my pain, every hug from me would leave you with a stain

– M.R.S

Sanity

Sometimes I don't want to write...
I get lost in these lines and sometimes I am scared they'll find me and
bring me back to sanity,
But the pen is my friend,
If I fixed me then he would cease to exist
And damn, that would make me a murderer
And it would be the worst to know that I am not the one that died
– M.R.S

Finish

When I take this pen thoughts of my death get written
If I threw it away that would mean the wrong person died
But I continue to write, not only for the pen's life but mine because I
have come to realize that I am nothing without the pain,
Any other feeling would be foreign to me
I continue to write because I know someone out there is feeling the
same.
They put the rope away and turned to my pain
Knowing we shared the same 4 a.m. to let out our pain keeps them
sane
So I continue to spiral and throw the pills away because I can't be
gone, because it's not only my story that ends. – **M.R.S**

Life jacket

So hurt from human beings, that you couldn't decide whether to follow your heart or let your mind take the wheel, now you cut so deep you found yourself drowning in your thoughts, and your heart decided it will no longer be your life jacket – **M.R.S**

Sender

I found myself in my suicidal thoughts,
The thoughts terrified me,
Not of my death...
But the reality that now I can never be alive ever again. -**M.R.S**

Lead

Lately I just don't know where to go
So I keep on this road in hopes to find my way
I don't know where I am headed,
But I got my fingers crossed
Looking to the cross for some guidance – **M.R.S**

Past

I think they broke the wrong parts of me because I am travelling with
a heavy heart hoping the blurredness of my eyes from crying can see
me through
Trusting my pain to lead us to our destination
I never left, but I find myself wanting to go back – **M.R.S**

Price

No light then, no light now,
Feeling blind because my eyes should be on the price
But my emotions took the wheel,
I am just praying that we're being led to Christ
Because if all they said about him is true then my peace is in sight
And if I don't make it through I heard his home is the price – **M.R.S**

Daughter

Couldn't right my wrongs, too late to repent
Got me think I am the daughter of a serpent - **M.R.S**

Soldier

Everyday feels like a war and when I close my eyes every night I pray to have lost the battle
But I breathe again in the morning and everyone is calling me a true warrior
But I am that soldier that wishes to never make it back home.
– M.R.S

Manual

The truth is...
We are not going to make it out of here alive
I always knew that,
I just never knew that I would die and live at the same time
I died a long time ago,
8 is such a young age to turn into a solid soul
I exist for the masses,
They say that my presence brings peace and love
For days on end my absence has been on my mind,
If my absence would just exist
They say they cannot be without me so I sit here on this bed tonight
writing a manual for them
The answer is simple...ignore my absence the same way you ignored my
presence. – **M.R.S**

Saint

Sometimes I feel that God did me wrong
But then I look back and I see I was no saint – **M.R.S**

Goodbye

I feel that my time here is up... – **M.R.S**

Spotlight

Sometimes I want to pick my phone up and make that call and ask for help
Went through my contact list but the number I was looking for was not in sight
Maybe because I didn't even know who to turn to
Got all these people telling me all I gotta do is reach out and they will help me out
But when standing eye to eye I can't seem to let it all out
My demons are telling me they don't want to be exposed
And the devil is telling me no one needs to know I am where he resides
So I put that phone down and I grab this pen, hoping my demons don't think that this is too much spotlight for one night – **M.R.S**

My song

Everyone is singing the song "I am here for you"
And I provide the lyrics to the verses with my pain
And they sing a chorus telling me my life isn't all that bad
So I left the recording booth and started searching in the streets for an unfamiliar face
I figured I talk to a stranger because the people that know me don't know and it upsets me!
So I turned off the song, went on set and put on a show, made them believe that I am doing okay
At the end of the show I searched for an unfamiliar face because these people provide their rock hard shoulders for me to cry on and so I figured I sit under a bridge with the homeless, they're staring at me wide eyed but they don't know that I also have less
Everyone talking to me about how blessed I am, but the stranger in the street was the only one that cared to ask if I was happy because what are blessings if my happiness is not granted?
What does it all mean, when you are the envy of a lot but you envy the lot?
I would give it all away if it meant I could sit with a stranger and talk about how filthy the world is – **M.R.S**

Help

I have always needed help...
On some days I needed love or space
But every day? I needed help – **M.R.S**

Trainees

My life has reached a point where if it can go wrong then it definitely will!
Damn, got me thinking the devil is training demons with my life
He has trainees running this mess!
So I stumble and fall as they strike again trying to please their master while he's telling them "show me what you got!"
So I got on my knees praying for new management and the devil told me he'd disown me and take the pain away
So I grabbed those pills and let the trainees have their way - **M.R.S**

Virtual

My therapist told me that I tell stories so much that I have lost touch
of reality
She said I had become the story and no longer the story teller
This was it...
The realization that everything I have made thus far was all fictitious,
the friends, the workload, the experiences...even the family
None of it was real!
I just ran with a storyline and somewhere along the line everyone
caught up
After all, I was known to be the author that brings tragedy to life
– M.R.S

Pretty boys

And the day just came when every thought made my heart race
Thinking of you in any light left me in the dark
Whether it was a good or bad thought it always ends in tears
Because I just can't grab the fact that we are a used to be
Damn...A has been
Like we just hit rock bottom and my breaking heart has me throwing
rocks your way
Sometimes I wish I throw enough to bury you,
Have you suffocate kinda like I did when you walked away from me
and make sure no other girl ever finds you
And on some days I want to save you from the hell I created
I know you won't turn to me once you catch your breath
But I still grab that shovel and dig you out for the next girl,
Because every girl deserves a pretty boy – **M.R.S**

Pie

I stopped running and let my demons catch up with me
I got so tired of fighting this pain,
So I threw the pills away and let them win
What's the combination to the safe?
I am finally valuable, somebody lock me away!
No room to move, no air coming in,
Suck the breath out of my lungs, let my face turn purple
Brain damage is the aim!
Anything to forget the path that led me to this hell
I know better than to believe these pills are gonna help me
Because I know they're prescribed to tame me
But I am no Richard parker and even on a good day I don't want any
piece of that pie – **M.R.S**

Quiet

I witnessed a murder...
Whenever I saw that stuff on the news I would always think
"Damn what a sight, to have to watch someone drop dead"
But oddly enough she didn't drop dead...
No gun went off,
No knife went in...
Hell the perpetrator was not even in sight!
All I heard was a whisper in the far distance telling her
"This is it, the end"
She turned pale,
Like those words meant the end of her life and not the end of the life
she shared with someone else.
She was terrified of going back to her old life because back then pain
she knew and a stranger came along and swooped her up and
introduced her to happiness
But the thing about consistency is that you have to maintain what you
introduce and that was just something the perpetrator failed to
produce
His words made her feel like her worth had been reduced
I saw the look in her eyes,
She was about to see what people see when they go to the light,
She was horrified, I could see she was light headed....
It must have been the memories and experiences she had come to
realize she'd have to let go
But she didn't go out just like that!
She reached for that razor and put up a fight
Every cut was deep enough to sink the enemy

I turned to her wondering if it mattered to her that she was bleeding
out,
I wondered if she realized that just one more cut then her and the
enemy will share the same fate,
Man I wanted nothing more than to bandage her up
A true queen wears a smile, whatever happened to her kingdom?
Because she can't even make up a frown
Her walls are decorated, but I am afraid they might fall down,
Her cuts are starting to sink her now
She whispered back "Can't you see I need you?"
And I saw it happen then and there...
I didn't know silence could kill. – **M.R.S**

Memory

I always think that I gotta protect my heart from you
So I think the best way is to stay away from you
But physical distance doesn't ruin emotional presence
As heavy as the load is...I carry you with me
I keep you in my heart, you're safer there
My mind can't make decisions
It's telling me to get rid of you but keeps the memories
All the time spent has turned into a journal
My brain documented the journey
And on some nights my heart adds a few edits and our ending is
somewhere along the lines of a happy ever after – **M.R.S**

Reality

My reality doesn't like to see me happy
So every time it throws a hurdle
I grab my pen and I imagine a place that makes sense
A place that keeps me from grabbing my throat and choking
Sometimes I think that the answers are on the other side because that
is where the big homie is looking from
I need an angel to come down and play me my ending because if hell is
where I am headed then being here makes no difference – **M.R.S**

In the future

Someday I hope to be left alone
No one expecting me to submit any assignments
No pressure to get a job
No need to hang around a few friends so you could take pics for the gram and make everyone believe you have it all figured out even though you're barely managing!
No requests to drop a pin and link
Talk about things that that make my heart bleed so you could use my pain to form a connection with the next
No "I am here for you"
Someday I hope to be left alone...even when I am free. – **M.R.S**

Karma

In the past I made decisions that I could not take back
I gave love that I didn't get back
I caused pain and karma clapped back – **M.R.S**

Hopscotch

The devil got a hold of me when I was ready to change
And with every fight I ended up with a new condition
My attempts to free myself from the devil just let to more demons
because they called it PTSD when I chose not to engage
They called it depression when they found me in tears
They called it bipolar when I didn't know which leg to stand on
So now I just hopscotch through life and maybe one day I can finally
put both my feet down – **M.R.S**

Wound

What is it all about?
Put it all on the table
Lay your cards down
Hold it! No poker faces allowed!
I am trying to see the real you
Let your scars bleed, I am sure there is a bandage here somewhere
You killed her didn't you?
Don't worry I got skeletons too,
But mine don't live in a closet, I carry them through
And I know you heard about my cuts,
I am ashamed to admit it but the razor saw me through
I couldn't turn to them I am sorry but they saw my blues and blew
Every shoulder I cried on ended up in a coffee shop laughing about
how I am not making it through
And my family? Even blood was not enough
And King? He didn't love me I called his bluff
So many are hungry for that dough so permission to use me for
sacrifice is granted. That is my only ticket out
I thought about that rope,
Hanging from a tree seemed like the way to go
But the coward in me just loosened that noose
Because a part of me feared I would end up on the news
I can't handle the fact that suicide will be the last statement I make
So I started writing, in case a thief came in the night and took my life
My final words will tell you how I wished to be gone
But stayed for you
So what is it all about?

Can't you see?

I breathe through wounds just so you can have me for another day

– M.R.S

Transportation

I figured I hide away but not from my demons because no matter how
far I go it's hard to get rid of them when my past is their
transportation and my mind is their home
I can only wish everyone can let me go through this alone – **M.R.S**

Time slot

I wish I could tell you that it gets better with time but my whole life I have waited for time to pass by but it seems I may be a second too late and a minute too far from my peace – **M.R.S**

New home

Nothing hurts more than not knowing what to do, knowing that you
tried it all but somehow nothing seems to work out
I had people tell me "let it work itself out"
So I put my problems out, told them "find yourself a new home"
I locked the door but every time I close my eyes I see them hovering
over me telling me to let them back in
They know no one who could take them
so I reached for that door and I let them stay
I don't know of anyone that can ever harbour what I have harboured
and my issues knew it too, so they refused to flee from me and got rid
of anything that might be a threat...happiness included – **M.R.S**

Needs

Maybe I am in need of a new start
A fresh book to write a new story
That part 1 to the best series
That first cry of an infant
That bamboo seed being planted...that's what I need – **M.R.S**

Flooded

I don't know how to heal
so I figured I dip my hands into everything
if I could do anything but feel then it meant I had healed – **M.R.S**

Prescription

I got to popping those pills,
hoping my pain drowns in my prescription
killing a piece of me that I no longer want to be part of me – **M.R.S**

Fair demons

My demons are fair you know?
During the day they flee from me and let me be a normal person
They let me laugh and get the day's work done
Hiding their existence from everyone around me so good that I
sometimes forget that I am carrying one of them through
I have tens of thousands of demons in my presence at night but during
the day they leave their least favourite behind and he watches me go
about my day making sure I don't expose what they do to me at night
When the dark comes they circle around me
They start whispering to me things about the past,
things I would like to forget and
if I shut my ears they start pulling on my body dragging it to the
medicine cabinet and daring me to OD
On some nights I agree
Maybe the pills are the answer
Maybe the pills will help me get rid of them
but then I realize if they go, I go too and it's the worst to know we're
all headed to the same hell – **M.R.S**

Sky

On some days I feel like I deserve it so I let it consume me,
I let the pain have its way with me and on some days I don't
understand why the universe felt that I deserved it so I hold on to my
pillow rocking back and forth hoping a sign would show up and make
me understand why I had to go through it – **M.R.S**

Dawn

This is it...the point I thought I would never reach
but it's true what they say about pain
You know? The fact that it hurts until you feel nothing
I had reached a point where I had accepted that tragedy was my life
I had accepted that this was not my story to tell but I had a role to play
Have you ever watched a story where there was just this one character
that was always in pain, seldom has lines but constantly in tears?
I just finally understood that the odds would never be in my favour
They say that things get better over time, somebody froze mine
They say that your darkest hour comes before your dawn...this has got
to be the longest night – **M.R.S**

Tomorrow

I stopped waiting for a better tomorrow and started accepting the worst today – **M.R.S**

Better

I had plans to be a better person,
but my past just wouldn't let me
it told me it goes wherever I go,
I could not leave it behind
so I carried it with me to my next destination
leaving no room for anything else because it took up all the space,
it was the same as yesterday
and I knew it will be the same tomorrow – **M.R.S**

Still...

I am always in pain
even when I smile a piece of me still bleeds – **M.R.S**

Illusions

Even when I feel like I am making it through, there is a piece of me that brings me back to what I thought I had freed myself from
– M.R.S

Otherwise

I am not one to point fingers
but when my mind lingers
I am Einstein with the equation
the math finally made sense...1 plus 1 = 2
so how come you weren't true?
breaking every second of the day and you know you are to blame
I am in pain and you put me here
the worst about all of it is you promised you wouldn't
and I had my doubts and you told me otherwise only for you to
convince me then go prove to me otherwise – **M.R.S**

Insert

I got on my knees trying to part with these demons
But now I am stuck between a rock and a hard place
I gotta ask for forgiveness on wrongs that made my heart race,
The devil whispers I have ran out of grace but he knows a place where
my demons belong
If I could just take that rope, the journey won't be long
So I kick that chair from under my feet hoping my family doesn't
think that I am wrong. – **M.R.S**

Young

I heard the good die young that means I am fucked because if I don't down these pills tonight then my death is not in sight. – **M.R.S**

King

I wish I could love myself the same way that I love him.
Maybe I would learn to let go of anything that harms me.
Helped him face his past yet I couldn't confront my own demons, told him he should let all the pain go yet mine stayed.
I knew he deserved somebody that understood so I picked his traits up...7 months later, I am a part of him and I wonder if he fears the old version of him fuelled the new version of me because I am toxic now and he is the angel I used to be.
Every wrong he made I tried to help him right it, every tear? My hands were ready to wipe away but now I sit in the dark letting my tears hit the ground because I can't even love me enough to wipe my own tears away.
I tried to get him to start a new life yet I couldn't even bring myself to start a new day, it's like I would risk it all for him even if the firing line is where my end begins as long as that is where his pain ends

– M.R.S

Breakthrough

My past is not an excuse for all this pain I still go through but my present is the hell I walkthrough to the future where there is no breakthrough – **M.R.S**

Heaven

My faith is at an all time low but when I am down, the heavens is where I look for a reminder to breathe – **M.R.S**

Residence

Don't leave me alone, my demons find me easier that way, when you're around I can at least put up a fight, because I don't want you to know that my mind is where the devil keeps his best soldiers and every day they promise to take up residence in my heart.
So stay...please don't let my heart turn cold – **M.R.S**

Similar

I am no different from those that left because just like them...I can't love me too – **M.R.S**

Locked away

They say I have come far but my demons laugh because they have me locked away in the past – **M.R.S**

Space

I have always needed love, but I needed space more.
I could be drowning but wish to be left alone.
On some days I need a hug but every day? I needed space, because it's
just hard to let anyone close to me now because I know they will soon
be gone and no matter who leaves the pain is always worse than before
and if one more person walks out of that door...
I will go too – **M.R.S**

Searching

I am still trying to heal.
I am still trying to understand why it's so hard to love myself.
I am still trying to talk myself out of fastening that noose.
I am still trying to get back to my youth.
I am still breathing through wounds.
My heart is still heavy.
I am still searching for a reason to live – **M.R.S**

Little girl

The little girl in me doesn't smile anymore she just sits and wonders why I haven't reached for that razor. – **M.R.S**

But this...

All I did was search for a better place, spent my whole life trying to find a new life, there had to be a better version of what I live, there had to be a version of me out there that felt anything but this
— M.R.S

Amnesia

I ran to the rope again...I am ashamed to admit it but it seems like the only way, the pain in my chest makes me feel like no one is really watching and the demons in my head keep telling me I can't hide forever, and if I ran faster they would catch up with me because I have a cross to carry, consequences of my past decisions have found their way to me,
I was stupid to think going on my knees meant I could amnesia my way past my mistakes and look forward to a brand new day because I know now, even if I burnt sage and prayed for better days I still need to pay my dues for past mistakes – **M.R.S**

•••

I am trying to be okay but it gets hard because for so long I just thought I wasn't able to – **M.R.S**

Muse

If I am being honest my childhood is the reason for all these pills that I abuse, and my present is a reason I seek a muse but I am scared I will never find a way so the past is where I reside looking for a piece of me that I lost but the future is telling me to let it all go, start afresh...learn to love myself again, but my past laughs because just like the people that used to love me, I can never love myself again

– M.R.S

No choice

I've been captured by my demons again and this time they chained my heart to my past, leaving me with no choice but to leave all of me there
– **M.R.S**

•••

I am scared I will never find a way, and every time I look at the ceiling
my heart is consoled by the thought of a rope and I am convinced, just
one more knife to my chest and my death will be this way
– **M.R.S**

Circle

It doesn't get better, it just gets normal...there is no progress, just a deceptive circle leading you back to your demons – **M.R.S**

Forgive me

I know it's no excuse but I am just a 20 year old trying to wipe the tears
of the 8 year old that died inside of me, so forgive me if it feels like I
am just not here with you...
I have journeyed into the past trying to convince that little girl to set
me free but she sits at the bottom of my heart telling me I can't
abandon her like everyone else so forgive me when I seem distant
today, I am just trying to be there for that little girl that died inside of
me while you assumed she grew up.
– M.R.S

Bamboo

I am just the seed that got washed away by the storm while everyone sits and waters my grave like i am the bamboo tree waiting to bloom –
M.R.S

World...of

I am running out of room, pain is just not something my heart can harbour anymore and I am scared if I let anybody close I might just drown them with me, I am sorry for this mess I made, I was just a kid trying to find love in this world of hate – **M.R.S**

Blessings

In the end it was a blessing...but for the most part it felt like a curse
– M.R.S

A better place

In some ways I am grateful for knocking on heaven's door because then I would have never left my hell, and my demons would have never left me alone...although the door remained closed...my demons knew now I was capable of finding a better place – **M.R.S**

???

I don't know if it's these pills or I am just numb – **M.R.S**

Psych

I often get asked how I feel and my response is always the same...I am on whatever my psychiatrist puts me on – **M.R.S**

Faded...

I honestly couldn't' tell you if i felt numb or it was the drugs,
my memory was starting to fade away,
I could barely remember the road that led me to this place,
it's like all events were falsified and I was locked away into paradise
because it was suddenly blissful to just exist,
made me forget that I had plans to be gone tomorrow, now I look
forward to the next day, because every morning a pill I take and a pill a
day meant I was getting further away from the pain that landed me
here. – **M.R.S**

Lessons

Somewhere along the road to insanity, there was a lesson there
– **M.R.S**

Invade

I was still trying to decide if feeling nothing at all was suddenly a
blessing or I had finally reached the epitome of hell,
I was now the devil's agent, no remorse, no conscience, no feelings, just
a demon that landed on earth feeling nothing at all,
I was convinced now more than ever that I belonged to the serpent
because angels feel it all and act accordingly, while demons feel
nothing and wander about searching for souls to invade and take over
just to feel something
– M.R.S

Found grace...

And the time just came...
I no longer wished to be the same as yesterday
So I got on my knees, this conversation has been a long time coming
Thinking back at what brought me here,
I know now I missed a step and fell from grace
I am just wishing my mother says a special prayer for me because I
don't know what to say to be okay
I don't know what to apologise for to be forgiven
I don't know what sin needs repentance
So I pray it all away,
The pain, the sin, the deceit, the journey that led me to this point
My heart's heavier than before,
Carrying myself and this organ that died but still beats,
I knew then that miracles still happened
Why else has the rope failed?
Why else where the pills not enough to check me out?
Why else was the razor not able to go deeper?
Undeserving...but his grace is still the same,
So I am certain this pain will disappear – **M.R.S**

The end

Don't miss out!

Visit the website below and you can sign up to receive emails whenever Millicent Segwane publishes a new book. There's no charge and no obligation.

https://books2read.com/r/B-A-YOBI-ETKLB

BOOKS 2 READ

Connecting independent readers to independent writers.

Also by Millicent Segwane

Ethereal
Machima
#FleshAside
From Her Heart To Her Grave
Only When The Mic Is On
Schooled by the Hustle
The Locksmith
The Thibela
Auctioned emotions
Presidential: a woman scorned
The kind of love that keeps a man 2
Love me like you promised
Notes To The Psych Ward